"SNAKES AND SUCH"

ALVIN SILVERSTEIN · VIRGINIA SILVERSTEIN · LAURA SILVERSTEIN NUNN

TWENTY-FIRST CENTURY BOOKS
BROOKFIELD, CONNECTICUT

Cover photograph courtesy of The National Audubon Society Collection/Photo Researchers

Photographs courtesy of Visuals Unlimited: pp. 6 (© D. Cavagnaro), 10 (© Jim Merli),
14 (© Rob Simpson), 18 (© Ken Lucas), 22 (© Jim Merli), 30 (© Ken Lucas);
Animals, Animals: pp. 26 (© Marian Bacon), 34 (© Joe McDonald), 38
(© Marian Bacon), 42 (© Zig Leszczynski)

Cover Design by Karen Quigley
Interior Design by Claire Fontaine

Library of Congress Cataloging-in-Publication Data
Silverstein, Alvin.
Snakes and such/by Alvin & Virginia Silverstein & Laura Silverstein Nunn.
p. cm. — (What a pet!)
Includes bibliographical references (p.   ) and Index.
Summary: Discusses the positive and negative aspects of keeping such creatures as boas
and pythons, chameleons, iguanas, turtles, frogs, and salamanders as pets.

ISBN 0-7613-3229-4 (lib. bdg.)
1. Reptiles as pets—Juvenile literature.   2. Amphibians as pets—Juvenile literature.   [1. Reptiles as pets.
2. Amphibians as pets.   3. Pets.]   I. Silverstein, Virginia B.   II. Nunn, Laura Silverstein.   III. Title.   IV. Series.

SF459.R4S55   1999
639.3'9—dc21   98-41305
                                                                                                                                   CIP
                                                                                                                                   AC

Published by Twenty-First Century Books
A Division of The Millbrook Press, Inc.
2 Old New Milford Road
Brookfield, CT 06804

CONTENTS

WHAT A PET!

THIS SERIES WILL GIVE you information about some well-known animals and some unusual ones. It will help you to select a pet suitable for your family and for where you live. It will also tell you about animals that should *not* be pets. It is important for you to understand that many people who work with animals are strongly opposed to keeping *any* wild creature as a pet.

People tend to want to keep exotic animals. But they forget that often it is illegal to have them as pets, or that they require a great deal of special care and will never really become good pets. A current fad of owning an exotic animal may quickly pass, and the animals suffer. Their owners may abandon them in an effort to return them to the wild, even though the animals can no longer survive there. Or they may languish in small cages without proper food and exercise.

Before selecting any animal as a pet, it is a good idea to learn as much as you can about it. This series will help you, and your local veterinarian and the ASPCA are good sources of information. You should also find out if it is endangered. Phone numbers for each state wildlife agency can be found on the Internet at

http://www.animalsforsale.com/states.htm

and you can get an updated list of endangered and threatened species on the Internet at

http://jjwww.fws.gov/r9endspp/endspp.html ["Endangered Species Home Page, U.S. Fish & Wildlife Service"]

Any pet is a big responsibility—*your* responsibility. The most important thing to keep in mind when selecting a pet is the welfare of the animal.

FAST FACTS

Scientific name	*Thamnophis sirtalis* (common garter snake) in Family Natricinae; *Heterodon nasicus* (western hognose snake) in Family Xenodontinae
Cost	Garter snakes $20 to $40. Others can cost hundreds of dollars.
Food	Most prefer to eat live food, including insects, worms, fish, frogs, toads, lizards, salamanders, newborn mice (pinkies), chicks, and rats. Larger species require mostly warm-blooded animals.
Housing	Smaller snakes do well in a 20 gallon (75.7 liter) aquarium tank. Bigger snakes will need a bigger tank. Tank should include a hiding place, a sturdy water bowl, a branch (if tree-dwelling), rocks, a heater, full-spectrum light bulbs.
Training	Can be tamed and handled, but use caution. Snakes, at some point, will bite. They cannot be trained with treats. Snakes eat when they feel like it.
Special notes	Owning poisonous snakes may be illegal in some states. Certain snakes may require permits. Like other reptiles, snakes may carry salmonella, which can cause illness in humans. Wash hands thoroughly after handling the pet.

STARTER SNAKES

SNAKES ARE AMONG the most feared animals in the world. Just the thought of snakes scares many people. But people who have pet snakes would say these animals are misunderstood. Contrary to popular belief, most snakes are really harmless.

Snakes are fascinating. They can be tamed and handled and admired for their complex and colorful patterns. They range from the common garter snake to huge pythons. These are not pets for everyone, though. Snakes have special needs. Some kinds of snakes are easier to care for than others. For a starter pet, it is best to get a small, mild-tempered snake—one that is *not* poisonous. Larger snakes, especially those over 8 feet (2.4 meters) long, should be left to more experienced snake owners.

COLD-BLOODED REPTILES

Snakes are reptiles. All reptiles are cold-blooded animals. That does not mean that their blood is always cold. It just means that they cannot warm themselves and maintain a constant body temperature the way mammals and birds do. That is why reptiles often bask in the sun, so they can warm up. If they do not get the warmth they need, they will get very sluggish, and may even die.

A UNIQUE GROUP OF REPTILES

Snakes are legless reptiles. But it wasn't always that way. Millions of years ago, snakes evolved from lizards. Like lizards, these ancient snakes had four legs. Because they preyed on animals that lived in burrows, the snakes had very little need for their limbs. Mutations (genetic changes) that resulted in shorter limbs did not hurt their chances to survive. In fact, the snakes that no longer had limbs had a more streamlined shape and were very successful in slithering through long, narrow burrows. Thus, over many, many generations, snakes developed into their present-day appearance and a new way of moving around.

What could be more amazing than the way snakes move across the ground? How *do* snakes move without legs? They move on their bellies. Muscles inside a snake's body expand and contract,

> **DID YOU KNOW?**
> Of the 2,400 species of snakes, 800 are venomous (poisonous), but only about 250 are actually dangerous to humans.

pulling it along the ground. The rougher the ground, the faster the snake can travel. It cannot move very well on smooth surfaces.

Snakes cannot hear because they do not have any ears. But they can tell when something is coming near because they feel vibrations in the ground through their bodies. They can feel a person's footsteps coming from many yards away, and since they are shy by nature, they can quickly dart away before you even see them.

A snake has a forked tongue that is constantly flicking in and out of its mouth. Contrary to popular belief, a snake's tongue will not sting you. Snakes use their tongue to smell. The tongue picks up scents and then brings them inside the mouth to two tiny pouches called the Jacobson's organ. This organ contains nerve endings that are very sensitive to smells. That is how snakes can locate food, find a mate, or spot an enemy. Snakes do have nostrils, but they use them only for breathing, not smelling.

All snakes have very sharp, needlelike teeth. They use them to grab their prey, but they cannot chew. They swallow their prey whole. Venomous snakes have fangs, long hollow teeth that contain poison called venom. A snake's venom is really used to control its prey so that it can safely swallow its meal. What do non-venomous snakes do? These snakes feed on smaller, less threatening prey, such as fish, frogs, or small lizards. So all they have to do is grab and swallow.

Snakes have amazing jaws. A snake can unhinge its jaws and open its mouth wide enough to swallow prey that is larger than the snake itself. It takes a while to digest such a big meal. Snakes do not have to eat as often as other animals do. Many snakes need to be fed only every two weeks, or even less often, depending on the size of the meal.

A snake grows throughout its entire life. But a snake's tough, scale-covered skin cannot stretch as the snake grows. So the snake has to shed its skin regularly in order to grow. (Lizards do, too.)

SNAKE PETS

In the wild, snakes can be found throughout the warmer regions all over the world. Some live in cold regions, too. Snakes can live in a variety of habitats: in the desert, in trees, on the ground, and even in the water.

When you get a snake of your very own, you need to know about its background to be able to take care of it properly. Does it live in trees? Does it burrow? How big will it get? Does it like to be handled?

These are some very important questions you need to answer before you get your pet. It may be hard to believe that the cute little baby snake you take home may grow to be 6 feet (1.8 meter) long. Indeed, snakes can vary greatly in size—from the wormlike Texas blind snake, which reaches no more than 11 inches (28 centimeters) to the reticulated python of Asia, which can grow to as much as 32 feet (nearly 10 meters) long, probably the longest snake in the world.

The common garter snake is a popular pet and is good for a beginner because it does not grow very big and is easy to care for. Garter snakes are common throughout North America. You may see them in gardens, which is why it is sometimes called the garden snake. The garter snake is usually olive brown with yellowish stripes and measures about 22 inches (56 centimeters) in length.

The western hognose snake is another popular pet. These snakes range from southern central Canada to Texas and northern Mexico. Their pointed snouts are upturned, looking very much like a hog's nose. The hognose snake may grow up to 35 inches (89 centimeters) long.

Hognose snakes are real characters. In the wild, they use trickery to fool their enemies. When a predator approaches, the hognose snake will raise its head and shake its tail, pretending to be a rattlesnake. It hisses loudly and puffs out its neck to look bigger. If that does not work, it plays dead. It turns over on its back, opens its mouth and sticks its tongue out. The inside of its mouth looks like rotting meat, and it smells like it, too. That is enough to scare away most enemies.

There are many other good starter snake pets, including certain kinds of kingsnakes, milk snakes, corn snakes, and ratsnakes. It is very important to research snakes before getting one. The decision to own a snake should not be taken lightly. No matter how "tame" your snake is, at some point it is likely to bite the hand that feeds it.

INTERNET RESOURCES
http://exoticpets.miningco.com/library/weekly/aa050298.htm "A Snake for a Pet?" by Lianne McLeod
http://fovea.retina.net/~gecko/herps/snakes/snake-care.html "Care Sheet for Snakes," by Paul Hollander
http://planetpets.simplenet.com/snakes.htm "A World of Snakes"
http://www.robinsfyi.com/snake.html "Snakes and Such" (including articles, snake humor, and links to snake sites, other reptiles, and amphibians)
http://www.sonic.net/~melissk/gartcare.html "Garter Snakes"
http://www.sonic.net/~melissk/king.html "Kingsnakes and Milksnakes," both by Melissa Kaplan

FAST FACTS

Scientific name	*Boa constrictor imperator* (common boa constrictor) in Family Boidae; *Boa constrictor constrictor* (red-tailed boa) in Family Boidae; *Lichanura trivirgata ssp.* (rosy boa) in Family Boidae; *Python regius* (ball python) in Boidae
Cost	Common boa $75; red-tailed boa $125; ball python $30
Food	Feeds primarily on warm-blooded animals such as rats, mice, rabbits, or other small mammals. Most snakes prefer live food but they can learn to take frozen mice or rats. Captive boas and pythons should be fed moderate amounts on a regular basis. Larger snakes should be fed larger meals every two weeks or so.
Housing	The cage should be at least two-thirds the length of the snake. For instance, a 2-foot (0.6-meter) cage is good for a 3-foot (0.9-meter) rosy boa; 4- to 6-foot (1.2- to 1.8-meter) for a 6- to 8-foot (1.8- to 2.4-meter) boa. Cage should include a hiding place, a sturdy water bowl, a branch (if tree-dwelling), rocks, a heater, and full-spectrum light bulbs.
Training	Can be tamed and handled, but use caution.
Special notes	Many places require permits for boas and pythons. Like other reptiles, snakes can carry salmonella.

BOAS AND PYTHONS

HOW WOULD YOU LIKE a 10-foot (3-meter) snake in your living room? Boas and pythons are famous for their enormous size. Though the sight of these very large snakes can be a little frightening, many snake owners say that boas and pythons are very calm and friendly and can make good pets.

Boas and pythons may make good pets for some people, but they should not be a first choice as a beginner pet. No matter how friendly big snakes may be, they can be very dangerous, especially to children. Snakes have been known to escape from their cages, and they sometimes cause harm.

THE CONSTRICTORS

Some snakes use their venomous fangs to kill prey. Other snakes use their sharp teeth just to catch their prey and then swallow it whole. But boas and pythons are constrictors—they constrict, or squeeze, their prey to death. To constrict a prey, the snake must first grab the animal with its long, sharp teeth. It then quickly wraps one or more coils of its body around the animal. Contrary to popular belief, a constrictor does not crush its victim's bones. It just holds its prey tightly and tightens its coils each time the prey exhales or relaxes its muscles. Finally the prey dies of suffocation. The boa or python then relaxes its coils and swallows the animal whole. Constrictors may mistake small children for prey, so children should *not* keep constrictors as pets. And, never take chances by draping a constrictor around your neck.

> **DID YOU KNOW?**
> A snake has very strong digestive juices in its stomach that can soften the bones and skin of prey that it swallows.

THE LIVES OF BOAS AND PYTHONS

Boa constrictors are found in the tropical parts of Central and South America. (Two species, the rosy boa and the rubber boa, can be found in the western United States.) Boas can live in a variety of habitats, including deserts, savannahs, woodlands, and rain forests. They may be tree dwellers, burrowers, or ground dwellers. The anaconda is the only kind of boa that lives in the water. Boas grow to an average length of 6 to 10 feet (1.8 to 3 meters), though some may grow much bigger.

Pythons can be found in the tropical parts of Asia, India, the East Indies, Africa, and Australia. Most pythons are ground dwellers, but they are also good climbers and good swimmers. Pythons also grow to an average length of 6 to 10 feet (1.8 to 3 meters), though some may grow much bigger.

Snakes have an amazing body structure. Hundreds of bones in their backbone allow them to twist and turn easily in many different directions. The reticulated python has 400 bones in its backbone; the average person has only 33. That is why a snake can coil its body and we cannot.

Boas and pythons feed primarily on warm-blooded animals. These snakes have little holes, or pits, between their eyes and nostrils. The pit organs can detect the heat of warm-blooded prey, such as mice or rats. These heat sensors can help a snake find food even in the dark.

BOA AND PYTHON PETS

Common boa constrictors and red-tailed boas are both popular boa pets because they are fairly calm animals and good feeders. These two boas are often confused. Boa pets that are sold as red-tailed boas are often just brightly colored common boa constrictors. The true red-tailed boas are a bit larger and much more attractive than common boa constrictors. The remarkable red-tailed boas are also more expensive.

World Champions

Remember that the reticulated python is the longest snake on record, growing to 32 feet (close to 10 meters). But in South America, the anaconda, the only water-dwelling boa, is the heaviest snake, with a body length of less than 30 feet (about 9 meters), a body width of 3 feet (0.9 meters), and weighing as much as 330 pounds (150 kilograms) or more.

The common boa constrictor ranges from 6 to 9 feet (1.8 to 2.7 meters) long. Red-tailed constrictors are heavier than common boas, reaching as much as 12 to 14 feet (3.7 to 4.3 meters) long, although the average is 9 to 10 feet (2.7 to 3 meters).

The rosy boa is said to be the ideal boa constrictor pet because it is small, attractive, and hardy. Rosy boas are much smaller than the average boa constrictors, growing to only 2 to 3 feet (0.6 to 0.9 meter). In the wild, rosy boas are found in southern California, western and southern Arizona, down into Baja and

Not a Snake

The slowworm, found in Europe, Asia, and North Africa, is a legless reptile that looks like a snake but is actually a lizard. It has movable eyelids, and—like many lizards—it sheds its tail if it is frightened. (It can grow a new tail, which may be shorter than before and have a stubby end, not a pointed one.)

northwestern Mexico. These small boa pets are also easy to handle and can live for 15 years or more.

The ball python, an African native, is a very popular pet species. The ball python is smaller than the average python, only 4 to 6 feet (1.2 to 1.8 meters) long. If you see a ball python roll up into a ball, that does not mean that it is calm and tame. Ball pythons roll up in a tight ball when they are frightened. They try to protect themselves by hiding their head in the center of the secure body coils.

Ball pythons are very picky eaters and are known for going for long periods without food. Despite the feeding problem, they are very hardy animals and can live to 20 years or more.

Ball pythons are in great demand, which puts a tremendous amount of pressure on the wild populations. Even though they have a slow reproduction rate, the ball pythons are the least expensive pythons in the market.

Taking care of a snake, especially a very large boa or python, is a huge responsibility. Beware of the possible dangers and, most of all, be informed.

DID YOU KNOW?
Boas and pythons can go for many months without food.

INTERNET RESOURCES

http://exoticpets.miningco.com/library/weekly/aa050298.htm "A Snake for a Pet?" by Lianne McLeod

http://fovea.retina.net/~gecko/herps/snakes/snake-care.html "Care Sheet for Snakes," by Paul Hollander

http://planetpets.simplenet.com/snakes.htm "A World of Snakes"

http://www.robinsfyi.com/snake.htm "Snakes and Such" (including articles, "So you think you want a snake?" and "Your Snake Went Out for a Change of Scenery—Finding Your Escaped Snake," plus snake humor and links to snake-sites, other reptiles, and amphibians)

http://www.robinsfyi.com/boa.htm "The Common Boa"

http://www.sonic.net/~melissk/rosy_boa.html "Rosy Boas"

http://www.sonic.net/~melissk/ball.html "Ball Pythons"

http://www.sonic.net/~melissk/coloburm.html "The Keeping of Large Pythons," all by Melissa Kaplan

FAST FACTS

Scientific name	*Anolis carolinensis* in Family Iguanidae in Order Squamata
Cost	Inexpensive, often $5 or so
Food	Live bait only: flies, crickets, grasshoppers, mealworms, spiders
Housing	At least a 20-gallon (75.7-liter) aquarium with a mesh lid covered tightly; should include a heater, full-spectrum light bulbs, rocks, twigs, branches, and leaves.
Training	Most anoles do not like to be handled and may become stressed; some may respond well if handled frequently.
Special notes	Like other reptiles, anoles can transmit salmonella; wash hands thoroughly after handling the pet.

GREEN ANOLE

ANOLES

WHO COULD RESIST A PET that changes color? Sometimes sold as "American chameleons" in pet stores, anoles can change color, but they are not really chameleons. In fact, they are just common lizards, closely related to iguanas. Anoles can be very entertaining pets; they are active creatures and you never know just when they will change color.

THE REPTILE REVOLUTION

About 300 million years ago, some ancestors of the anoles took a giant step: They were the first reptiles—vertebrates (animals with backbones) that were able to live completely on land. Their ancestors, the amphibians, had to remain close to water and laid their eggs in the water. The first reptiles, however, had skin that was covered with

a protective layer of scales, made of a tough substance somewhat like our fingernails. The scaly skin kept their bodies from drying out. A second reptile

Not Much of a Chameleon

Compared to a real chameleon, an anole's ability to change colors is very limited—it can change only from bright green to dark brown and back again. Contrary to popular belief, anoles do not change their color to blend into their surroundings. An anole will not automatically match a tree branch it is sitting on or a colorful pattern on your shirt. Instead, these lizards change their color depending on the light, the temperature, and their mood.

Anoles are brown if they are sleeping or cold; they are bright green if they are warm and active. A brown color helps an anole to warm up because dark colors absorb heat. A pale green color reflects light and helps it to cool down. Male anoles may turn brown when defending their territories. Sick anoles turn dark brown but do not change back to green.

"invention" was an egg that contained a food supply (yolk) for the developing young and was wrapped in a baglike covering. Reptile eggs did not have to hatch out and develop in the water. They could be laid under rocks or in holes in the ground. The babies that developed inside these cozy sacs hatched out as completely formed miniature adults, ready to run about and eat and grow.

The early reptiles, which looked something like the lizards of today, were very successful in the struggle for life on the land. In fact, they spread out and developed into many different forms, including the giant dinosaurs that ruled the earth for more than 100 million years. All the dinosaurs are gone now, but four main branches of reptiles have survived: turtles, crocodilians (crocodiles and alligators), snakes, and lizards such as the anoles.

AN ANOLE'S LIFE

In the wild, anoles can be found in the southeastern United States and South America. Only the green anole is native to the United States. These lizards are very common from North Carolina down to Florida, over to Texas, Mississippi, Arkansas, and Tennessee. For people living in these parts, anoles are easy to spot. They can be found in bushes, small trees—but not above 15 feet (4.6 meters) tall—rock walls, woods, and around people's houses.

Anoles are diurnal animals—that is, they are active during the day. As their name suggests, green anoles are mostly green. They grow to 5 to 8 inches (13 to 20 centimeters) long, including the tail, which is often longer than the body length.

Green anoles are arboreal animals (tree-dwellers), but are more likely to live in bushes rather than trees so that they can scurry around on the ground. They are great climbers. In fact, anoles have amazing toes, which are flattened with ridges and tiny hooks at the ends. The surface of their toes works something like a Velcro fastener, helping anoles to climb up and over stones walls, hang upside down on a leaf, or even walk up and down a glass window. (So if you keep pet anoles in a glass aquarium, make sure the lid fits on tightly.) These lively lizards can also jump short distances, from branch to branch.

Anoles have a very distinctive characteristic: the male's very colorful throat sac, called a dewlap. This colorful fold of skin turns bright red or orange when the male is defending its territory against other males. Males may also put on a display of push-ups and head bobs to scare off intruders. These scare tactics do not always work, sometimes leading to a fierce battle. Male anoles may also show off their colorful dewlaps to impress females during courtship.

Many female anoles have a distinctive characteristic of their own: a white, almost zipper-looking stripe down their back.

ANOLE PETS

The green anole is the species you are likely to see in pet stores. Anoles are quite inexpensive, costing only a few dollars. However, they are often considered "disposable pets" because of the low cost and because they usually live for only 2 years.

Anoles can live alone or in groups. Two or more males should not be housed together, though, because they are so territorial. They are likely to fight. A male anole can live with females, however.

In the wild, anoles often lie on rocks, sunning themselves. Sunshine is so important that without it, they would die. In a home for a pet anole, a full-spectrum lightbulb (sold in pet shops and garden supply stores) can be used to substitute for the sun. Anoles also need warmth, with an average temperature around 78° to 80°F (25.6° to 26.7°C), and a sunning spot about 85° to 90°F (29.4° to 32.2°C). In anoles' wild habitat, it gets cooler at night; for pet anoles the night-time temperature can be kept at 68°F (20°C). The housing for these pets should also include rocks, twigs, and small tree branches for sunning and climbing.

It is important to keep their home moist and humid. Anoles will not drink out of a water dish, so they need water misting every day. They often lap up the water droplets from leaves or the sides of the aquarium.

Anoles can make very interesting pets. But many do not like to be handled and may become stressed. An angry or scared anole can and will bite. Some anoles may become tame if they are handled frequently and very carefully.

INTERNET RESOURCES
http://www.apci.net/~sirac/anoles.htm "The American Chameleon: Proper Care of Green Anoles"

http://ceismc.gatech.edu/zooary/zoo/reptiles/anole.html "Green Anoles"

http://www.retina.net/gecko/herps/lizards/anoles.html "Green Anole Care In Captivity," by Dr. Michael Corn

http://www.reptilemall.com/anoles.html "Green Anoles," by Melissa Kaplan

FAST FACTS

Scientific name	*Chamaeleo jacksonii* (Jackson's chameleon) in Family Chamaeleontidae
Cost	Females about $70, males about $90
Food	Must eat live food: crickets, mealworms, flies, moths, roaches; multivitamin supplements are available. Frequent misting gives chameleons drinking water.
Housing	At least a 20-gallon (75.7-liter) aquarium. (Bigger is better, especially for larger chameleons.) Should include a heater, full-spectrum light bulbs, rocks, twigs, branches, and leaves.
Training	May be stressed if handled too much
Special notes	Like other reptiles, chameleons can transmit salmonella infections. Wash hands thoroughly after handling the pet.

CHAMELEONS

CHAMELEONS ARE THE REAL color-changing champions of the reptile world. These remarkable reptiles can change not just from brown to green and back, but to really wild colors and patterns. Chameleons can make very interesting pets, but they are not for everyone. They are very delicate, and many pet chameleons die because they are not cared for properly.

OLD WORLD CHAMELEONS

True chameleons, or Old World chameleons, are found in Africa, Madagascar (a large island off the east coast of Africa), India, and in the south of Spain. They are tree-dwelling reptiles and are very awkward on the ground. The size and appearance of chameleons can vary greatly among the more than one hundred species that exist. Chameleons range in length from only about 3 inches (7.6 centimeters) long to over 2 feet (61 centimeters).

Color-Changing Champions

The word chameleon is often used to describe someone who is very changeable, switching appearance or behavior to blend in. Actually, some chameleons do not change color, but many can produce striking color changes—from pale green to bright green, yellow, orange, red, black, and sometimes blue. More than one hundred different color and pattern variations have been observed for the common chameleon, Chamaeleo chamaeleon.

The color changes may help a chameleon to blend into its surroundings, but it usually changes color for a variety of other reasons: to regulate body temperature, in response to light or darkness, and to attract a mate. To keep warm, chameleons turn dark colors that absorb sunlight; turning light helps keep them cool. A chameleon under stress—from an injury, perhaps, or in a dispute with another chameleon—usually shows a distinctive pattern with dark colors. When calm and contented, the same chameleon will be lighter, with a less distinct pattern or none at all.

Looking at a chameleon, it is hard to imagine how people could confuse anoles with these very unusual-looking creatures. Chameleons have a very narrow body and a dinosaur-like face. Some chameleons have horns on their heads. Their bulging eyes each move around independently. One eye can see what is going on straight ahead, while the other eye checks out what is happening behind the chameleon. When it spots prey, both eyes zero in on the target. The chameleon flings out its extremely long tongue and, in a third of a second, catches the insect with the sticky tip of its tongue. A chameleon's tail is another interesting feature—it curls at the end and is often used like a hand to grasp tree branches. A chameleon may use its tail to help it escape from predators. If a snake or another reptile comes too close, the chameleon will suddenly drop to the ground (unharmed), or use its tail to quickly grab onto another branch. Unlike the tails of other lizards, a chameleon's tail will not break off.

Although most other lizards move quickly, chameleons move very slowly. They may take a minute to walk twelve steps along a branch. Chameleons are even slow when they hunt insects. A chameleon may stay in one spot for hours, while its eyes are constantly looking for prey to come nearby. When it finally spots an insect, the chameleon creeps very slowly and quietly towards the victim. The chameleon looks like part of the tree until it is too late, and the insect is quickly slurped up.

CHAMELEON PETS

Chameleons are a very delicate species. Large numbers of chameleons that are brought to the United States die or get sick from the difficult trip. They do not get the proper care and become stressed. Chameleons sold in pet stores often do not make very good pets. These pets usually do not live long. It is best to buy a chameleon pet from a well-known breeder. Breeders usually take special care of their chameleon stock.

The three-horned chameleon, or Jackson's chameleon, is one of the most popular chameleon pets. It is much hardier than most other chameleons. The Jackson's chameleon is probably the first chameleon to be successfully bred in captivity. These reptiles are native to Mount Meru and Mount Kenya in Africa. In 1972, however, 36 animals were brought to Hawaii to be sold in pet stores. To help the chameleons recover from the stress of the trip, the owner released them into the backyard of his pet shop. The chameleons eventually produced a wild population of Jackson's chameleon in Hawaii. Nearly all the Jackson's chameleons sold as pets in the United States today are descendants of this Hawaiian population.

A male Jackson's chameleon has three horns, making it look like a little triceratops dinosaur. The female, however, may have three horns, only one, or none at all. Jackson's chameleons grow to about 10 inches (25.4 centimeters) long.

Chameleons are solitary animals. Keeping more than one chameleon in a cage may cause stress for the animals and lead to death.

Jackson's chameleons, like other true chameleons, need cooler temperatures than you might expect. During the day, it should be about 75° to 80°F (about 24° to 27°C). At higher temperatures, the chameleon could die. At night, the temperature should be lowered to about 60°F (15.6°C). Chameleons also need frequent water misting to provide them with drinking water and to keep humidity in the air.

Though chameleons are fascinating creatures, their special needs make them a better choice for experienced pet owners, not beginners.

INTERNET RESOURCES

http://orsp1.adm.binghamton.edu/~steve/CCS/ "Chameleon Conservation Society" site (with information on chameleon classification, species, frequently asked questions about care and breeding, movies to download, and links)

http://www.skypoint.com/members/mikefry/title.html "Chameleons," by Michael Fry (a very comprehensive site with information on choosing, housing, and feeding pet chameleons, coping with problems, and descriptions of several species)

http://freespace.virgin.net/chameleon.hh/cham.htm "Some Information about Chameleons," by Zach Twist

http://www.chias.org/www/edu/gen/animals/Chameleon.html "Jackson's Chameleon (*Chamaeleo jacksonii*)"

FAST FACTS

Scientific name	Family Gekkonidae. *Eublepharis macularius* (leopard gecko); *Gekko gecko* (Tokay gecko); *Madagascariensis grandis* (giant day gecko)
Cost	$20 to $200, depending on species
Food	Must eat live food: crickets, mealworms, flies, moths, cockroaches. Should provide water bowl, but not all geckos will drink from water bowls, so frequent water misting may be needed instead.
Housing	At least a 20-gallon (75.7-liter) aquarium. Should include full-spectrum light bulbs, rocks, twigs, branches, leaves.
Training	May be stressed if handled too much. May bite if annoyed or scared. If handled frequently and properly, leopard geckos may tolerate handling.
Special notes	Like other reptile pets, geckos can transmit salmonella infections. Wash hands thoroughly after handling the pet.

LEOPARD GECKO

GECKOS

MOST LIZARDS ARE QUIET animals, making nothing more than hissing sounds. But not geckos. Many people believe that geckos sound like they are saying the word "gecko." That is how they got their name. Geckos may also make hissing sounds and chirping sounds to communicate.

Geckos are fascinating reptiles. They are fun to watch. But if you are looking for a pet that you can play with, geckos may not be for you. They do not like to be handled very much, and they may bite.

REPTILE RAGE

Geckos have sparked people's curiosity since the "reptile rage" in the 1980s. Before that time, few people had ever heard of geckos. But pet stores were selling them like crazy. Many people wanted these geckos not just as pets, but as a kind of pest control. People who live in New York and other big cities have problems with cockroaches, insects that infest buildings and can cause health problems. Since geckos love insects, these lizards seemed like an ideal solution. The Tokay gecko became the top choice.

The Tokay, native to southeast Asia, is very large—about 1 foot (0.3 meter) long—and very fierce. You may often see the Tokay keeping its mouth open, ready to bite at any moment. And its bite really hurts—the Tokay hangs on tight, twists and turns, and can tear the skin and draw blood. Needless to say, these geckos do not make good pets, but many people still use them as patrolling exterminators. Tokays can eat as many as a couple of hundred cockroaches in a single day, but once their food source is gone, they may starve. A Tokay gecko cannot take care of itself in a person's home. And letting a Tokay gecko run around loose in the house is really not a good idea.

THE LIFE OF A GECKO

In the wild, geckos can be found in warm climates all over the world. The gecko family is very large, including more than 700 species. This big family is so var-

DID YOU KNOW?

Day geckos are well-known diurnal geckos. They have a much greater need for basking in the sun (or full-spectrum artificial lighting) than nocturnal geckos.

ied that it is hard to make general statements about them. For instance, most geckos are active at night (nocturnal) or at dawn and dusk (crepuscular). But some geckos are active during the day (diurnal). Some geckos are tree dwellers, while others live on the ground.

Geckos range from 3 to 15 inches (7.6 to 38 centimeters) long. Some species have an ordinary-looking dull brown color. Other geckos have more exciting colors—yellow, orange, green—and can be solid, striped, or spotted.

The eyes of many nocturnal geckos have narrow pupils in the center, similar to a cat's. But the gecko's pupils are shaped like little waves, compared to the straight ones of a cat's eyes. Diurnal geckos have round pupils. At night, the

Like Windshield Wipers

Some gecko species do not have any eyelids. Instead, the eyes are protected by a thin cover. Your eyelids keep dirt from getting into your eyes. These geckos clean the dirt from their eyes by using their long tongue to lick them clean.

gecko's pupils widen to let light in so it can see in the dark. By day, the pupils turn into a row of three or four tiny dots to decrease the light coming in.

Geckos are great climbers. Their feet have large toe pads that are covered with long, tiny hairlike scales that hold tightly onto any surface. They can easily run up a wall, walk up windows, and even cling upside down on a ceiling.

Geckos are also famous for their ability to drop their tails to escape from predators. The predators are too busy watching the twitching tail to notice the gecko making a quick getaway. The tail eventually grows

DID YOU KNOW?

A gecko sometimes will grow two or three tails to replace one that has been lost.

back, but it may not be the same color or even the same length as the original one. When a gecko drops its tail, it loses the food and water that is stored in it.

GECKO PETS

The leopard gecko is one of the most common gecko pets. Leopard geckos have a much better temperament than most geckos, and sometimes they do not mind being handled. They rarely bite. They are also much hardier than other geckos and, when cared for properly, can live up to 10 years or more. Leopard geckos do not make loud sounds like other geckos, but they will hiss or chirp when scared or angry.

Native to Pakistan, leopard geckos grow to about 8 inches (20 centimeters) long. They are very attractive reptiles, yellow with brown or black dots. Generally speaking, geckos are very territorial, and two males placed in the same cage will fight. (Day geckos are much more territorial than other geckos.) Keeping one male with females is acceptable.

Geckos make wonderful display pets. They are not recommended for handling because many geckos can bite. Most geckos may only prick your finger, but Tokay geckos can make a real wound. So a basic rule for gecko owners is: look but don't touch.

DID YOU KNOW?
Like other reptiles, leopard geckos shed their skin. But their skin does not come off in pieces. They bite their skin and eat it to get vitamins from it.

INTERNET RESOURCES

http://www.pathfinder.com/PetPath/Exotic/Breeds/REPTAM/GECKO/GECKO.html "Geckos" (article with gecko sounds and a movie to download)

http://www.simplynet.net/reptile/general.html "Gecko Garden" (general information, care sheets, pictures, and links)

http://www.acmepet.com/reptile/library/gecko.html "Leopard Gecko FAQ"

http://www.geocities.com/RainForest/7917/leopard_gecko.html "Leopard Gecko"

http://www.pythons.com/lg-care.html "Leopard Gecko Care Sheet," by Alan & Billie Zulich

http://www.geckoworld.com/~gecko/docs/leopard.html "Leopard Gecko Care Sheet," by Chris Norman

http://www.ionet.net/~gregc/daygecko.html "Day Gecko Information"

http://www.ionet.net/~gregc/pcare.html "Phelsuma 'Day Gecko' Care Sheet," by Greg Christenson

FAST FACTS

Scientific name	*Iguana iguana* (green iguana) in Family Iguanidae
Cost	About $10 to $20
Food	Plant-eating; diet may include romaine lettuce (*not* iceberg, which lacks good nutrients), kale, zucchini, broccoli, grapes, apples, bananas. Provide a water bowl. (If large enough, the iguana wili bathe in it, so it may need to be cleaned out frequently.)
Housing	Start out with a 30- to 50-gallon (114- to 189-liter) aquarium for young iguanas. As the iguana grows into an adult, provide a bigger cage. The cage should include full-spectrum light bulbs, rocks, hot rocks, heating pads, twigs, branches, and leaves. Mist frequently to provide humidity.
Training	May be stressed if handled too much. May bite if annoyed or scared. If handled frequently and properly, it may become tame. Some can learn to walk on a harness, or sit on a person's shoulder. Some can learn to eat from a person's hand. Some may learn to be paper-trained.
Special notes	Many iguanas carry salmonella, which can cause illness in humans. Wash hands thoroughly after handling the pet.

GREEN IGUANA

IGUANAS

WHAT WOULD IT BE LIKE to have a pet dinosaur? Dinosaurs may be extinct, but today's iguanas are descendants of the Iguanadon—a dinosaur that roamed the land millions of years ago. So having a pet iguana is like owning a piece of our prehistory.

Iguanas are the most popular reptile pets in the United States. Unfortunately, however, thousands of iguanas die each year as a result of stress they experience while being imported into this country. Many more die because they are not cared for properly. It is very important to learn about iguanas and their needs before owning one.

AN IGUANA'S LIFE

Iguanas can be found in Central and South America and the Caribbean islands. They are tree-dwelling lizards, but they also do well roaming on the ground. Iguanas are great climbers and have very sharp, strong claws that help them hold onto tree trunks and branches.

Iguanas are also great swimmers. They often climb trees that are hanging over water. If frightened, an iguana will fall from a tree branch into the water and quickly swim away from danger or hide out among some aquatic plants until the coast is clear. It may use its long, strong tail to give it a boost through the water. If there is no water down below, the iguana will drop from a tree to the ground and land on all fours, the way a cat does, without getting hurt. It then immediately rushes off for cover.

DID YOU KNOW?

The name *iguana* refers to the largest members of the iguanid family. This family contains more than 700 species. They are a varied group, including anoles, horned lizards, chuckwallas, basilisks, and fence lizards.

IGUANA PETS

Green iguanas are the most popular iguana pets. You may not be able to resist that cute baby iguana in the pet store. It is only about 7 inches (about 18 centimeters) long. But you may not realize that these cute little lizards could grow

DID YOU KNOW?
An iguana can stay under-water for up to 30 minutes!

to a length of 6 feet (1.8 meter) in four to five years! The very long tail makes up about two thirds of the length. The iguana's tail is very strong, and it whips it around if it is angry. So don't get in the way of an iguana's lashing tail—it can really hurt.

Young iguanas are bright green. Adults have a dull green to grayish color, which gets darker with age. Males are generally larger and brighter than females. An iguana has toothlike spines that go from the back of the neck all the way down to the top part of its tail. It may also have a large dewlap, typically seen on males as a warning to other males to "come no closer." Males may also show off their dewlaps to the females during courting rituals. By nature, iguanas are very shy animals, but some can be tamed. You must be very gentle when handling them. To tame an iguana, you have to make it feel safe. Like people, iguanas are indi-

Watch Out for the Tail

Iguanas do not drop their tails as easily as other reptiles do. While other lizards drop their tail as a defense against predators, iguanas will do it only as a last resort. So never grab an iguana's—you could injure it.

viduals. Some like being handled, others do not. And if an iguana does not want to do something, it won't. Owners have trained iguanas to eat out of their hand, sit on their shoulder, and walk on a special kind of leash. Iguanas can even be paper-trained. Some people let their iguanas run loose in the house. This may not be a good idea for a couple of reasons: The iguana could get hurt, and finding it could be a problem. Also, iguanas that are raised in a cage tend to be easier to tame. But iguanas should never be confined to a cage all the time. A tame iguana needs special attention.

Iguanas are diurnal reptiles and need the warmth of the sun to stay in good health. Special full-spectrum lighting that includes ultraviolet rays must be provided. When the weather is warm enough, take your pet iguana for a walk outside for at least an hour to soak up the sun.

Iguanas are solitary animals. The males are very territorial and may become aggressive. Females generally make better pets.

Having an iguana is probably the closest thing to owning a dinosaur. But taking care of these

DID YOU KNOW?
Iguanas may become very active and aggressive after warming up in direct sunlight. A normally tame iguana will not want to be handled at such times. Let it calm down for a few hours out of the sun before you try to pick it up again.

lizards is a big responsibility. It requires a lot of time and patience. A strong, healthy iguana can be a longtime companion with a lifespan of over 20 years!

INTERNET RESOURCES

http://www.sonic.net/~melissk/ig_care.html "Melissa Kaplan's Giant Green Iguana Information Collection" (links to more than 150 articles on green iguanas and related subjects, including a 26-page article on "Iguana Care, Feeding, and Socialization," reptile veterinarians, herpetological societies and resources, conservation issues, pet store and animal regulations, and care information on other iguanid lizards)

http://www.baskingspot.com/iguanas/igbook/index.html "The Iguana Pages," by Jennifer Swofford (a manual, "The Complete Guide to Keeping Giant Green Iguanas in Captivity," an article, "Should I Get an Iguana?" plus lists of resources, information on other iguanids, and links to iguana sites)

http://www.bestintexas.com/pets/listiguanasforpets.html "Pet Iguanas Require Special Care" by Robyn Horton of Kansas State University News Service

http://www.majsoft.com/gen_facts.html "Iguan-O-Rama: All About Iguanas"

http://www.pclink.com/dkelley/igcare.htm "Iguana Care"

http://members.aol.com/ignews/life.html#anchor1952401 "A Day in the Life," "What Is a Folivore?" (nutrition), and "Iguana Names"

FAST FACTS

Scientific name	*Basiliscus plumifrons* (green basilisk) in Family Corytophanidae; *Physignathus cocincinus* (Chinese water dragon) and *Physignathus lesueuri* (Australian water dragon) in Family Agamidae
Cost	Basilisks $20 to $50; Chinese water dragons about $25 (imported) or a little more for captive-bred hatchlings; Australian water dragons $75 to $150
Food	Preferably live foods, including crickets, grasshoppers, mealworms, and newborn mice (pinkies); also vegetables (flowers, dandelion leaves, and shredded lettuce) and fruit (bananas, strawberries, and melons)
Housing	Adults should be kept in at least 55-gallon (208-liter) tanks. Bottom of tank should be filled with 12 to 18 inches (30 to 46 centimeters) of water. Should also include twigs, branches, leaves, and rocks. For basking, full-spectrum light bulbs, hot rocks, and heating pads. Mist frequently to provide humidity.
Training	Water dragons tolerate handling better than basilisks do. Always be gentle. Water dragons can become tame and eat from the owner's hand. Basilisks are very skittish and are not likely to become tame.
Special notes	Like other reptiles, water dragons and basilisks may carry salmonella, which can cause illness in humans. Always wash hands after handling pet reptiles.

BASILISK

WATER DRAGONS AND BASILISKS

WHAT DO WATER DRAGONS and basilisks have in common? They are both linked to an ancient mythological creature, the dragon. The water dragon was named after the legendary fire-breathing reptile. The basilisk got its name from a medieval legend describing a beast that looked like a cross between a dragon and a rooster. With a glance or a breath, the legendary basilisk could turn a person into stone.

The historical link between water dragons and basilisks is not the only thing these intriguing lizards have in common. Even though they belong to different families, they have some rather similar characteristics. Water dragons and basilisks are becoming increasingly popular pets as more people learn about these interesting creatures.

WATER DRAGONS

The green water dragon, also called the Chinese water dragon, is a popular choice among lizard pets. A green water dragon looks very much like an iguana, although it is not as large. The green water dragon can grow up to 3 feet (nearly 1 meter) long, about two thirds of which is the tail. It has a lush green color with a touch of blue and pink around the throat. Like the iguana, the green water dragon has a spiny crest that runs from the back of the neck down to the tail. Males have a somewhat larger and brighter-colored crest than females.

Various kinds of water dragons live in the forests of Asia, Africa, and Australia. The green water dragons of China and southeast Asia spend much of the time in trees that overhang water. These lizards are great swimmers and quickly drop into the water to escape predators. They are also comfortable on the ground and can run very fast to escape enemies or chase prey. They often run on only their hind legs.

Coming from tropical areas, green water dragons need plenty of warmth when they are kept as pets. The brown water dragons from Australia are less sensitive to the cold. Some lizard owners say they are calmer and hardier than the green water dragons. They are some-

DID YOU KNOW?
Water dragons will not breed unless they have had a "winter rest" of about two months at cooler temperatures.

what scarcer and more expensive, however; Australia now has strict regulations forbidding the capture and export of native wildlife, so the only brown water dragons available are the descendants of animals owned by breeders in other countries before the strict rules went into effect.

Male water dragons are very territorial. Males should never be housed together, but one can live happily with a group of females.

Young water dragons can be tamed if they are handled frequently. They may crawl up your arm, and you may be able to feed them by hand. Water dragons have a lifespan of 3 to 10 years or more.

Lookalike Cousins

The green water dragon looks amazingly like the green iguana. It might seem that these two species are very closely related, but actually they are only rather distant cousins. They developed in different parts of the world and belong to different families. The water dragon is a member of the Agamidae family from Southeast Asia, and the iguana, from the Iguanidae family, comes from Central and South America, a whole ocean away.

But their habitats are quite similar—both live in tropical rain forests. The ancestors of each lizard adapted to the similar conditions of their homes and wound up as lookalikes. Scientists call this convergent evolution.

BASILISKS

The green basilisk is popular for its remarkable appearance. The adult male has a finlike crest on its back and tail and a double crest on its head, called a "head plume." (In fact, this lizard is sometimes called the "plumed basilisk.") The basilisk grows to about 3 feet (close to 1 meter) long, most of which is the tail. Its base color is green with bluish tints on its sides and dark stripes all over its body.

The green basilisk can be found in the tropical forests of Central America, from Guatemala to Costa Rica. Like green water dragons, green basilisks are tree-dwelling lizards that live on branches hanging over water. They too will drop into the water to escape from danger. But they do something unique—they walk on water! Their back feet have scaled flaps of skin between the toes. When running on water, they extend these flaps, making the feet almost float on the water. The basilisks have to run very fast; if they slow down or stop, they will sink. Fortunately, they are excellent swimmers, and will quickly swim away. (Because of their ability to "walk on water," these basilisks are often called "Jesus lizards" in Latin America.)

Males are extremely territorial and should not be housed together. They are likely to have violent fights, which can result in serious injuries. Males do well living with a group of females, however.

Basilisks are much more easily frightened than water dragons. When basilisks are startled, they go wild and will bang right into the glass aquarium, hurting their snouts. Because of their nervous temperament, handling of pet basilisks should be kept to a minimum.

INTERNET RESOURCES

http://www.pathfinder.com/PetPath/Exotic/Breeds/REPTAM/WATERDR/WATERDR.html "Water Dragons"

http://members.aol.com/msnick1/waterdragons.html "Chinese Water Dragons, Physignathus cocincinus"

http://www.icomm.ca/dragon/dragoncr.htm "Care of the Chinese Water Dragon," by Tricia Power

http://home.earthlink.net/~timo2/waterdragon.html "The Brown Water Dragon, Physignathus L. Lesueurii," by Bert Langerwerf of AGAMA

http://www.sonic.net/~melissk/basilisk.html "Basilisks: Captive Care & Breeding," by Peter Paterno

FAST FACTS

Scientific name	*Terrapene carolina* (North American box turtle); *Trachemys scipta elegans* (red-eared slider) in Family Pipidae. *Chrysemys picta* (painted turtle) in Family Discoglossidae.
Cost	$10 to $20 for common species; up to hundreds for rarer ones
Food	Land turtles: plant foods, including banana, apple, melons, grapes, squash, mustard greens, kale, dandelion leaves; also some meat, such as earthworms or snails. Aquatic turtles: diet should include both fruits and vegetables, and also lean dog food or earthworms.
Housing	Aquatic turtles: a 20-gallon (75.7-liter) aquarium tank, with some water for swimming and a rock for land area, plus plants and vegetation. Land turtles: May need a larger tank, with water in a dish.
Training	Most turtles do not like to be handled, but some may become comfortable with their owner and feed from the owner's hand.
Special notes	It is illegal in some states to collect certain species of turtles from the wild, and some species are threatened or endangered. Also, turtles may carry salmonella, which can cause illness in humans. Wash hands after handling them.

EASTERN PAINTED TURTLE

TURTLES

HAVE YOU EVER WATCHED a turtle creeping in the grass in your backyard? Or maybe you saw one trying to cross a road. It seems to take forever for a turtle to walk from one place to another. Turtles are famous for being slow-moving, and yet they are fascinating to watch. Turtles can be fun pets, and they can live for a very long time. Many pet turtles die after only a year or two, though, because pet owners often do not know how to take care of their turtles properly.

SUIT OF ARMOR

The turtle is the only reptile that has an outer shell. This shell is a protective suit of armor that shields the turtle's soft body. Many turtle species can pull their head and legs inside the shell and hide from their enemies. A box turtle can close its shell so tightly that its upper and lower shells cannot be separated, even with a knife blade.

> ### What's in a Name?
>
> *Is it a turtle, a tortoise, or a terrapin? How do you know which is which? Actually, any reptile with a shell is called a turtle. The term turtle is just a general name for this group of animals. More specifically, however, turtles usually spend most of their time in the water, and have flat shells. Tortoises spend most of their time on land and have a more rounded top shell. (There are exceptions, however: For example, box turtles spend most of their time on land.) In England,* turtle *is often used to describe marine species, while most freshwater species are called terrapins.*

Turtles cannot slip in and out of their shells. The shell is a part of the animal's body, attached to its skeleton. As the turtle grows, the shell grows with it. If the shell is injured, the turtle is harmed as well. The shell is very sturdy, but it can break if the turtle falls or is dropped from a height, and then the turtle will probably die. Painting a turtle's shell is also harmful because it keeps the shell from growing.

A TURTLE'S LIFE

Only 220 species of turtles exist in the world today, one tenth the number of living snakes and lizards. They may not be as diverse as other reptiles, but turtles are very hardy and adaptable animals. In fact, they come from the oldest branch of the reptile family tree, which separated from the main group close to 300 million years ago—about 100 million years before the age of the dinosaurs. Their body plan was so successful that it has changed very little in the past 200 million years.

Depending on the species, turtles can live in a wide variety of habitats, from hot deserts to the open seas. They also vary greatly in size—from the tiny musk

Some Smart Turtles

Turtles are not the smartest animals, but the wood turtle is probably the most intelligent species. In laboratory experiments, using food rewards, wood turtles learned to run a maze almost as fast as laboratory rats. Wood turtles make good pets, but they are not widely available and are therefore very expensive.

turtle, less than 5 inches (13 centimeters) long, to the enormous marine leatherback; the largest on record was more than 9 feet (nearly 3 meters) long and weighed over a ton (more than 900 kilograms). The largest land-dwelling turtle is the Galápagos turtle, which grows to more than 4 feet (1.2 meters) and weighs over 550 pounds (about 250 kilograms).

Turtles are specially adapted to where they live. Land turtles, or tortoises, have short, stubby legs good for walking on land. Aquatic turtles have webbed feet that help them swim in the water.

All turtles need sunlight. The sunlight produces vitamin D, which keeps their shells and bones from becoming weak. But they will become ill if they have too much sun.

DID YOU KNOW?

Turtles continue to grow all their lives and live longer than any other animal. One of the oldest turtles was believed to be 170 years old when it fell off a wall and died in 1918.

Turtles do not have any teeth, but the edges of their jaws are very sharp. They can slice through most plants and animals. They can even gnaw through wood. Although not usually aggressive, a turtle may bite your finger if it is annoyed. Turtles also have very sharp claws and can scratch you.

Most turtles are very shy and solitary animals and will hide in their shells at the first sign of danger. But some species, such as snapping turtles, cannot pull their head and legs into their shell. A snapping turtle defends itself by attacking, quickly "snapping" at its enemies.

> ## Protecting the Turtles
>
> *Box turtles were more popular in the pet industry a few years ago than they are today. The main reason is that they have been overcollected from the wild. Box turtles are extremely popular in Europe, and thousands die during shipping overseas because they are jammed into the packing containers, with no food or water; others die from mistreatment. Box turtles were recently added to the Convention on the International Trade in Endangered Species (CITES) treaty as a threatened species, and strict laws now regulate their export.*

TURTLE PETS

Until the mid-1970s, turtles were very popular pets. But in 1975 the Food and Drug Administration (FDA) banned the sale of turtles less than 4 inches in diameter in the United States. Turtles may carry salmonella bacteria, which can cause salmonella poisoning. (In 1972 alone, there were almost 300,000 reported cases of turtle-linked salmonella poisonings.) The FDA ruling was based on the fact that salmonella could easily be spread if young children put these cute little turtle pets in their mouths. Since any turtle can carry salmonella, no matter what the size, it is important to wash your hands after touching a pet turtle.

It was not until the late 1980s that the popularity of the Teenage Mutant Ninja Turtles turned turtle pets into a craze once again.

There is a variety of turtle pets to choose from. One of the most popular pets is the red-eared slider. It has a red or orange ear-patch, which makes it easy to identify. The painted turtle is another favorite pet. It is an attractive turtle with red markings on the edges of the shells, and yellow stripes on its head and neck.

INTERNET RESOURCES

http://www.halcyon.com/slavens/blinks.html#Turtles "Herp Links," by Frank & Kate Slavens (hundreds of links to pages about reptiles and amphibians, with a special section on turtles)

http://www.geocities.com/Heartland/Plains/3550/index.html "Turtle Pages," by Jeff Dawson (articles including "What is a Turtle?" "Evolution of Turtles," "Anatomy of a Turtle," information on painted turtles, Eastern and Western box turtles, sliders, and snapping turtles, plus fun stuff like a "Turtle Trivia" quiz and turtle cursors for Windows 95)

http://www.altern.com/reslider/res.html "Reslider's Swamp" (red-eared slider and links to turtle sites, including some in French and Spanish)

http://www.geocities.com/RainForest/Vines/5504/ "Box Turtle Care and Conservation Web Page," by Tess Cook (including an on-line care book, photos, and links to articles on box turtle natural history and care)

F A S T   F A C T S

Scientific name	*Xenopus laevis* (African clawed frog); *Hymenochirus sp.* (dwarf clawed frogs) in Family Pipidae. *Bombina maxima* (Oriental fire-bellied toad) in Family Discoglossidae. *Litoria caerulea* (White's tree frog) in Family Hylidae
Cost	Frogs $10 to $50; tree frogs $6 to $50; toads $2 to $40
Food	Many species need live food, including crickets, fruit flies, grasshoppers, spiders, earthworms, moths. Some small species may only need food flakes (sold in pet stores).
Housing	Most species are content in 20-gallon (75.7-liter) aquarium tanks. Terrestrial tank for land frogs and toads includes branch, vegetation, bowl of water. Aquatic tank for totally aquatic frogs is water-filled tank with vegetation and gravel and rocks on bottom. Half-and-half tank includes half water and half land with vegetation and rocks. Arboreal tank for tree frogs is taller, with branches for climbing, plants, a bowl of water.
Training	Most species do not like to be handled and may never get used to it.
Special notes	It may be illegal in some states to collect certain species of frogs and toads from the wild. Frogs and toads may carry salmonella, which can cause illness in humans.

FIRE-BELLIED TOAD

FROGS AND TOADS

HOW MANY PETS CAN you think of that do not have a tail? This "tailless" trait is one of the things that makes frogs and toads such unique pets. It is also the main characteristic scientists use in classifying frogs and toads. The group to which they belong is called Anura, meaning "tailless."

Some people think that owning a pet frog or toad will be as much fun as watching them hop around in the backyard or near a pond or a lake. It certainly can be fascinating to watch frog eggs hatch in an aquarium. First they are little fishlike tadpoles that eat plant food. Then they go through an amazing series of changes called metamorphosis. They grow legs, lose their tail, and turn into hopping animals that eat bugs. After they grow up, though, pet frogs or toads may not be as exciting as you would expect. Some species are rather active, but others may just sit around all day.

A DOUBLE LIFE

Frogs and toads are amphibians. *Amphibian* comes from a Greek word that means "double life." Frogs and toads do have a kind of double life—they can live on land and in the water. Scientists believe that amphibians developed millions of years ago as a link between fish and reptiles. Ancient amphibians had heads and tails like fish, but they had lungs for breathing air and legs for moving around on land. They returned to the water to lay their eggs. As generations went by, some amphibians lost their tails and developed into frogs and toads. A few lost their legs and became snakelike. Millions of years later, some of the amphibians evolved into reptiles. The reptiles could lay their eggs on land and spend their whole lives out of the water.

FROG OR TOAD?

What's the difference between frogs and toads? In general, frogs are smooth and slimy and live in the water. Toads live on land and have a bumpy, drier skin. But you can't always tell a frog from a toad just by looking at it. Some toads live in the water, and some frogs live on land. For instance, tree frogs spend most of their lives in trees and rarely go to the water except to breed. The Surinam toad spends its entire life in water and would never survive on land without any access to water.

A frog's smooth, slimy skin needs to stay moist to keep it from drying out and to help it breathe in the water. (Its lungs are not good enough to do all the work of breathing.) Frogs drink water by absorbing it through their skin. With long back legs with webbed feet, frogs are excellent jumpers and Olympic-class swimmers.

A toad's rough and bumpy skin is much drier than a frog's skin. Toads spend most of the time on land rather than in the water. They breathe through their lungs, so their skin does not need to be moist. Toads have short legs, so they usually walk or make short hops.

Don't Kiss a Frog!

The fairytale princess had to kiss a frog to find her prince, but animal experts would not recommend it. Many frog and toad species have poison glands in their skin and will release this white, poisonous mixture when they are frightened. If you touch this poison and it gets into your mouth, you could get very sick. The poison of some frogs and toads can actually kill a person. So always wash your hands after handling a frog or toad.

FROG AND TOAD LIVES

Frogs and toads can vary greatly in size. Depending on the species, they may range from less than half an inch to almost a foot (from 1 to 30 centimeters) long. While many frogs and toads are green or brown, some are very colorful: yellow,

orange, red, or even blue. In the wild, frogs that are green or brown are most likely adapted for camouflage, hiding by blending into their surroundings. Frogs with colorful markings are most likely advertising that they are poisonous, trying to warn predators to stay away.

Frogs and toads have vocal cords in their throats and can make many different kinds of sounds. Both males and females can croak, but males are louder than females. Males often use their loud voices to court a mate.

Frogs and toads have a long, sticky tongue that they can fling out in an instant to catch insects. Their tongues have taste buds like yours, and they will spit out anything that tastes bad.

More than one frog can be placed in a single aquarium, but never put small frogs in with larger frogs. The larger frogs will probably eat the smaller ones.

FROG AND TOAD PETS

People keep various kinds of frogs and toads as pets. One popular pet (except in Oregon and California, where it is illegal) is the African clawed frog. It will grow to about 5 inches (12.7 centimeters) long. Its color may range from gray to brown, and even albinos are becoming popular. The African clawed frog is completely aquatic. It cannot survive outside the water. It has smooth, slippery skin, with large, webbed back feet and clawed front legs. These frogs can be aggressive and should not be grouped with fish or smaller frogs. The African dwarf clawed frog may be a better choice for beginner pet owners. It is much smaller and less aggressive than the African clawed frog.

The Oriental fire-bellied toad is another popular pet. It is very attractive, with a bright green and black top skin and a bright red and black patterned belly. Although it grows to only 2 inches (5 centimeters) long, it needs plenty of space: a 10-gallon (38-liter) aquarium for two adults. These toads are very active and can be really fun to watch.

The White's tree frog is another popular pet for beginners. It is much calmer than other frogs and may even sit on your shoulder or your hand for a while. Tree frogs need more care than other frog or toad pets. The White's tree frog lives best in high humidity, so its home needs to be sprayed with water frequently.

INTERNET RESOURCES

http://www.teleport.com/~dstroy/frogland.html "Frogland" (vivid pictures and plenty of information about frog natural history, pet frogs, "Weird Frog Facts," coloring book, and a section on "Save Our Frogs!")

http://www.csu.edu.au/faculty/commerce/account/frogs/frog.htm "The Somewhat Amusing World of Frogs," by Craig Latham

http://www.mnet.com/~dstroy/info/first.html "Your First Frog"

http://www.online.discovery.com:80/DCO/doc/1012/world/nature/frog/treefrogs1.html "Froggy Went A-Courtin'" (frog life cycle in color photos and text)

FAST FACTS

Scientific name	*Ambystoma mexicanum* (Mexican axolotl) in Family Ambystomatidae; *Salamandra salamandra* (fire salamander) in Family Salamandridae; *Typhlonectes natans* (caecilian) in Family Typhlonectes
Cost	About $5 to $40
Food	Give a varied diet of living insects including crickets, mealworms, cockroaches, grasshoppers, flies, earthworms.
Housing	Most species are content in 20-gallon (75.7-liter) aquarium tanks. Aquatic tanks, where no land is needed, require only gravel and plants. Semi-aquatic tanks should include land and water access with gravel, plants, moss, log, branch. Terrestrial tank should include plants, moss, rock or log, a dish of water. Mist to maintain humidity.
Training	Most species do not like to be handled. The axolotl is fairly calm, though.
Special notes	Collecting salamanders from the wild may be illegal in some states because their numbers have declined greatly in recent years.

MEXICAN AXOLOTL

SALAMANDERS AND NEWTS

YOU PROBABLY KNOW MORE about frogs and toads than you do about salamanders. That is not surprising. Little is known about salamanders and newts because they are such secretive creatures.

> ### Salamander or Newt?
>
> *What's the difference between salamanders and newts? Actually, the two words are really just used to describe different types of salamander. Basically, the term salamander generally describes any tailed amphibian. A newt, also known as an eft, is any salamander species that lives on land from late summer through the winter, but becomes aquatic in the spring to reproduce. Newts then return to the land when the breeding season is over.*

Keeping a salamander or newt pet is a great way to watch how these animals live and to learn about their daily habits. But these are very delicate animals, and handling should be kept to a minimum.

LIZARDLIKE AMPHIBIANS

Salamanders look like little lizards. In fact, *salamander* comes from a Greek word that means "a lizardlike animal." But salamanders are not lizards. They are amphibians, just like frogs and toads. As amphibians, salamanders spend their lives both on land and in water. But unlike their tailless amphibian cousins, salamanders are amphibians with tails.

At first glance, it is easy to see how people may mistake salamanders for lizards; both have a long body, four short legs, and a long tail. But look a little closer and the differences become obvious. Salamanders have smooth, moist skin and soft toes and live in or near water. Lizards, on the other hand, have scales and claws and live in dry, warm places.

THE NIGHT LIFE

Salamanders are nocturnal animals; they hide during the day and come out at night. They are not easy to find because they are very shy and secretive. They live in cool, moist places—in wet leaves, in rotting logs, or under rocks. While most species spend part of their lives on land and part in the water, some salamanders spend their whole lives in the water.

Salamanders can be found in North and South America, Europe, North Africa, and Asia. Unlike lizards, these amphibians prefer to live in cooler regions. They are rarely found in tropical or southern regions. When the temperature gets too warm, they burrow into the ground. Although most salamanders can withstand very cool temperatures, they will hibernate when the temperature gets really cold.

Most salamanders range from 3 to 12 inches (7.6 to 30.5 centimeters) long, including the tail. The Asian giant salamander, found in Japan, is the largest species in the world, growing up to 5 feet (1.5 meters) long. Salamanders come in many different colors and patterns, including red, gray, orange, yellow, blue, brown, green, and black. Like frogs and toads, the salamander's skin is moist and slimy, to help it breathe.

Salamanders, like most amphibians, breed in the water. Salamanders go through several stages, similar to frogs and toads. Some time after the female lays her eggs in the water, young salamanders, called larvae, emerge from the eggs. Salamander larvae are somewhat different from the tadpoles of frogs. The larvae have obvious feathery external gills (the gills that tadpoles use to breathe are internal, like those of fish), and the front legs develop before the back ones (the opposite in frogs). Also, tadpoles feed completely on algae and other vegetation, while larvae are carnivorous (meat eaters) and eat all the tiny water insects they can find. Eventually, the young salamanders move onto land, where they continue to develop into the adult form. During metamorphosis, the frog loses its tail, but the salamander does not.

Salamanders do not have voices like frogs and toads. They do not really make sounds to communicate, but they may make little noises like coughs, grunts, or squeaks. Salamanders do not have eardrums, but they can "hear" by feeling vibrations through their forelegs and lower jaw.

SALAMANDER PETS

Salamanders are very fragile animals. They do not like to be handled and easily become stressed. Like lizards, salamanders can also drop their tails, especially if they are handled too harshly. But fortunately, the tails, or any other body parts, will grow back.

The Mexican axolotl is probably the most widely kept salamander species and is a great choice for beginner pet owners. Axolotls have been captive-bred for so many years that they are almost domesticated. They are less likely to get stressed than other salamanders.

Axolotls grow to about 7 to 8 inches (18 to 20 centimeters), although some can reach 10 inches (25 centimeters). Axolotls may be a dark sooty brown color with black spots and blotches, albino, golden, or olive in color.

Unlike most other salamanders, the axolotl spends its entire life in the water. It is known as the Peter Pan of the salamanders in that it never grows up. It does not go through metamorphosis like other salamanders. It stays as a larva throughout its life. It can even breed as a larva.

The fire salamander is another popular salamander pet. The fire salamander is valued for its colorful appearance: jet black with bright yellow or orange spots, blotches, or stripes.

People are also fascinated by the story behind the fire salamander's name. A long time ago in Europe, people believed these salamanders were born of fire. Of course, this is not true. But because of their secretive nature, these salamanders were rarely seen in the wild, so few people even knew they existed. When old logs were brought inside to throw into the fireplace, the heat from the fire drove the salamanders out from their resting place. The only time people saw these salamanders was when they built a fire. These brightly colored salamanders were the most recognizable, and therefore, were falsely given the name fire salamanders. This salamander's bright colors act as a warning to enemies that it contains poison glands. So make sure you wash your hands if you touch a pet fire salamander.

> ## DID YOU KNOW?
> Salamanders release poisons from their skin as a means of defense, just like frogs and toads. So always wash your hands if you do touch a salamander. These poisons have been known to make people very sick.

Legless Amphibians

*A relatively unknown amphibian, called the caecilian, is not like its amphibian relatives. It has no legs! The caecilian looks like a worm. One species (*Typhlonectes natans*) makes a great aquarium pet and is sold in U.S. pet stores.*

INTERNET RESOURCES

http://www.users.interport.net/~spiff/main.html "Newt & Salamander's Homepage" (care sheets, pictures, resources, links)

http://www.accent.net/kaymur/salamr2a.htm "An Introduction to Salamanders"

http://alienexplorer.com/ecology/p144.html "Salamanders (Overview)"

http://www.pathfinder.com/PetPath/Exotic/Breeds/REPTAM/SALAMAN/SALAMAN.html "Salamanders" (including sounds and movie to download)

NOT A PET!

DEEP IN THE SEWERS of New York City, it is said, monster alligators prowl, feeding on rats and unwary maintenance workers. They were originally pets that were flushed down the toilet when their owners decided they were too much trouble. This story is not true, of course. It's just a kind of modern myth. But it has a message. People who buy pets without thinking enough beforehand often get more than they expected or want to cope with. Those cute little "baby alligators" (which usually are actually caimans) can soon grow into big reptiles that are bad-tempered and dangerous. In general, crocodilians (alligators, crocodiles, and their relatives) are *not* good pet animals. Poisonous snakes and very large reptiles are also bad choices, especially as pets for children.

What about the other reptiles? Reading about the animals in this book, you have probably noticed that they are not really domesticated. Many do not like to be handled, even when they have had time to get used to their owner. They can be fascinating to watch, but difficult to care for properly. If you want a pet that is warm and cuddly and responsive, then reptiles are *not* for you.

Another concern about reptiles and amphibians is that many of them carry a very contagious disease germ called salmonella. This is a bacterium that can be found in the animal's feces and can spread to humans when the pet is handled. Salmonella poisoning can make you sick with diarrhea, dehydration, stomach cramps, a high fever, or even worse. So *you must carefully wash your hands after handling a reptile or amphibian pet.*

If you decide you really do want a pet reptile or amphibian, where will you get it? Many herpetologists (people who study reptiles and amphibians) first became interested in these animals after catching some in their wild habitat and "adopting" them. It may not seem harmful to take an individual lizard or snake out of its natural home, but now we realize that wild animals are part of communities of life that exist in a delicate balance. Taking a frog from a pond, for example, might lead to the survival of more mosquitoes. And if a lot of animals are caught for the pet trade, whole species may be put in danger of extinction. This is already happening. So buy only captive-bred reptiles and amphibians, raised by reputable breeders who know the species and its needs. Besides not encouraging the capture of wildlife, you will be more likely to get a healthy pet.

Remember also that many localities do not allow certain animals to be kept, or require pet owners to obtain special permits or licenses. You can find out the regulations for your area by calling your state wildlife agency.

If your pet develops health problems, you may discover that the average veterinarian does not have much experience with reptiles or amphibians. You can find a directory of vets specializing in "herps," listed according to geographical location, at the website of the Association of Reptilian and Amphibian Veterinarians (ARAV): **http://www.arav.org/**

FOR FURTHER INFORMATION

Note: Before attempting to keep a kind of pet that is new to you, it is a good idea to read one or more pet manuals about that species. Check your local library, pet shop, or bookstore. Search for information on the species on the Internet.

BOOKS

Alderton, David. *The Exotic Pet Survival Manual.* Hauppage, NY: Barron's Educational Series, 1997.

Burn, Barbara. *A Practical Guide to Impractical Pets.* NY: Howell Book House, 1997.

Coburn, John. *Amphibians Today.* Neptune, NJ: T.F.H. Publications, 1997.

Donati, Annabelle. *Reptiles and Amphibians,* (A Golden Book). NY: Western Publishing Company, 1992.

Messonnier, Shawn. *Exotic Pets: A Veterinary Guide for Owners.* Plano, TX: Wordware Publishing, 1995.

Parker, Steve. *Awesome Amphibians.* Austin, TX: Raintree Steck-Vaughn, 1994.

Siino, Betsy Sikora. *You Want WHAT for a Pet?!* NY: Howell Book House, 1996.

INTERNET RESOURCES

http://www.nwlink.com/~pawprint/petparts_b4ubuy.html "Before You Buy" (things to consider before getting a pet)

http://ww.petstation.com/repamp/ "Reptile & Amphibian Magazine" ONLINE.

http://www.sonic.net/~melissk/parent.html "So, you think you want a reptile?" (recommendations and warnings for prospective reptile owners)

http://www.sonic.net/~melissk/kid.html "So, your folks won't let you have a reptile. . ." (advice for responsible kids who want a reptile pet)

INDEX

Page numbers in *italics* refer to illustrations.